PLANT:

A Military Spouse's Guide to Cultivating Life

Eugenia R. Gardner, Ph.D.

PLANT:

A Military Spouse's Guide to Cultivating Life

Published by Johnson Tribe Publishing, LLC Atlanta, GA

Manufactured in the United States of America

Cataloging-in-Publication data for this book is available from the Library of Congress

ISBN: 978-1-7352637-9-3

FIRST EDITION –

Illustrations: AugustPride, LLC

Editing: WesCourt Advisors

USA $29.99

Dedication

To men, women and children who faithfully
serve alongside our service men and women.

Acknowledgements

This book is a celebration of our life together. Thank you to my beloved husband, El "Red-Tail" Gardner, for always holding my hand.

Thank you Corinne Shannon Choice and Elaine A. Foster for instilling in me the joy of gardening and the confidence to share my voice and story.

Thanks also to my friends and colleagues, who read the manuscript at different stages, as it evolved from a seed to shoot, from a flower to bountiful garden.

A heart-felt thank you to Sandi Jefferson, Mary McMillian, Naomi Brooks, and Brigadier General Julia Jeter Cleckley, USA (Ret.) for showing me the way.

Special thanks to Dr. Adair White-Johnson, for sharing your guidance; and thank you Erin Minitner and Monroe A. Anderson, Jr., for sharing your creativity on these pages.

"Every perfect gift comes from above..."

Photography: Erin Minter Photography ©
Cover Photography: Monroe A. Anderson, Jr. ©
Back Cover Photography: Portia Wiggins Photography ©

TABLE OF CONTENTS

INTRODUCTION

There are combat boots at my front door.

Nothing in my childhood or education prepared me to enter the unique and peculiar sisterhood of military spouses. My father's service in the Air Force began and ended long before I was born. Nevertheless, two days after our wedding, my husband and I packed up his Ford Explorer and drove to our first home in Tuskegee, Alabama, near Maxwell Air Force Base. So, I began my induction into a new community, an environment steeped with tradition, a culture, and language that I needed to learn and understand quickly. From experiencing frequent Permanent Change of Station (PCS) moves to shopping at the Commissary (grocery store), to goodbyes at the airport, to being called my husband's "dependent," I had a great deal to learn and many adjustments to make.

As a new bride, I was anxious to support my husband and the Airmen who served with him. I was also eager to start my new job as the vice president of communications and marketing at Tuskegee University. I had recently completed my doctoral studies, and I was looking forward to working in a prestigious academic environment. Almost as soon as we got settled, my husband received new orders, and we packed up and moved again. I quit my job, and we drove to our next duty station. While we always landed in welcoming communities, over time, the frequent moves and deployments began to impact my career, my sense of stability, and my happiness. I constantly felt like I was starting over.

During happy and stressful times, I find that I retreat to my garden. All of my academic graduations have been celebrated in garden receptions. I was married under a wisteria arch in a public garden in Cincinnati, Ohio. Every year for my birthday, my girlfriends and I have a wine and paint party in my garden. I enjoy the simple solitude and silence of being in gardens. I don't wear protective gloves when I garden. I like to feel the dirt, mulch, and plant roots with my bare hands. I love the smell of the earth as much as I like the scent of lavender and sage. The garden is where I pray, talk to God, and talk to myself. It's the place where I can listen. Bees, butterflies, dragonflies, and hummingbirds thrill me when they come to visit my garden. I was working in the garden when the idea of writing this book occurred to me. No matter where the Air Force sends us, it's not home until a terra cotta pot appears with flowers.

We had just made an extremely stressful and exhausting PCS move from Washington, D.C. to Stuttgart, Germany. Our household goods wouldn't arrive for months. My husband was TDY (temporary duty); I had time on my hands. It was summer, so I was trying to create a garden on top of our garage because it was the only sunny spot in the yard. While I was rooting around with the weeds and dirt, scriptures would come to my mind, and I would run in the house and write them down.

After a lot of stops and starts, I came to realize that I was creating a lovely vibrant garden that was my life.

Some of my closest relationships, most cherished moments, and deepest heartbreaks resulted from my experiences as a military spouse and military community member. September 11, 2001 and ongoing military engagements, along with the advent of social media, have led to more awareness, resources, and opportunities for military spouses and military families than any other time in our nation's history. The military spouse community is full of dynamic, intelligent, savvy people who are active in all walks of life and engaged in the military community and our broader society. Looking at demographic and societal changes, I expect the military spouse community to become more diverse, multi-dimensional, and more present in all areas of discourse and society.

It's been 15 years since we married in that hidden garden in Cincinnati. Today, I am the founder and Chief Executive Officer of my marketing and communications consultancy, CommunisPR, which allows me to contribute economically to my family and my community's well being. As a professional leadership coach, I've worked with other spouses and entrepreneurs as they've pursued their goals. It wasn't easy getting here, but it wasn't necessarily hard either.

I wrote this book to foster a dialogue with military spouses about how we remain resilient and pursue our personal goals and aspirations within the military community. In sharing my story of how I overcame obstacles and setbacks to launch my successful consultancy, I hope to engage military spouses in experiences that allow them to envision and create more fulfilling experiences and opportunities.

I've developed a mnemonic to outline the concepts presented in this book. It applies to the notion of our lives being like gardens. Essentially, we are going to PLANT to ensure we achieve our goals and experience full futures.

Admittedly, for military community members to think about planting is hard because we spend so much time uprooting our lives and families. To me, if we want to grow, we have to plant something. Once we plant something, we have to tend to and nurture it so that it will grow. This concept applies whether you want to grow hydrangeas or to grow as a person by pursuing your goals and dreams.

PLANT

T R A N S F O R M A T I O N   P R O C E S S©

PREPARING

Aligning with values

LEVERAGE

Engaging Core Strengths

Investing in Relationships

ACTION

Setting Goals

Implementing MAP

NAVIGATE OBSTACLES

Addressing obstacles and challenges

TRANSFORMATION

Attaining Goals

Sharing Wisdom

Developing New Goals

Eugenia Gardner

EUGENIAGARDNER.COM

I discuss military-based resources throughout the discussion. I've included these resources because they've applied to my situation, and they've proven effective for thousands of service members and families.

I've structured this book as a 90-day resource guide that will allow you to create and begin implementing an action plan, referred to as a MAP (My Action Plan) in the guide. Throughout these pages, we are going to explore how our values, goal-setting, and action planning can help us achieve our goals, remain resilient, and maintain our careers while managing the rigors and frequent situational changes resulting from military lifestyles. We will explore how military spouses can build and sustain support networks and leverage resources to live full lives regardless of where in the world we are stationed. Through this discussion, I hope military spouses are equipped and empowered to begin planting and nurturing their gardens. Together, as a community, we will grow where we are planted.

Each section includes scriptures that found their way to me when I was working in the garden. I've added "Stepping Stone" activities, so you can apply some of the strategies discussed to ensure you are navigating and moving towards your goals and desired outcomes. I've also included additional resources, references, and activities that will allow you to "Dig Deeper" into the topics and skills presented. At the end of each chapter, there are gratitude moments to give you the opportunity to journal and reflect on, celebrate, and acknowledge your accomplishments and progress.

As the sun begins to set on my husband's military service career, I invite you to join me in the garden.

PREPARE

"Still others fell on fertile soil, and they produced a crop that was thirty, sixty, and even a hundred times as much as had been planted."

Matthew 13:8 (NKJV)

As a new gardener, I underestimated the importance of soil and the environment's impact on the vitality and growth of my plants. Preparing soil isn't the most exciting part of gardening, but it is probably one of the most critical aspects of creating a bountiful garden. No matter what I plant in my garden, nothing will grow unless I plant in healthy soil. If the soil doesn't have the right balance of nourishing elements, the plants will struggle to reach their full potential and bloom.

Achieving a flourishing garden requires understanding your soil's composition, allowing you to create a nurturing and supporting environment for plant growth. I, seemingly, always begin my garden beds by standing in weeds that reach my knees. Invariably, the soil is full of rocks and hard red clay. Usually, I have to dig a few 12 to 15 inches deep holes to see and feel the composition of my soil. Preparing the soil can be hard and messy work. Time and energy are required to develop a foundation for planting and an eventual harvest. I have to amend and change the soil by adding organic matter like compost or manure, shredded leaves, and peat moss. Still, I till and mix the soil anyway because I want a colorful and vibrant garden that I can enjoy year-round. With a deep breath and determination, I haul 50-liter bags of compost, soil, and mulch to create the nurturing and conducive environment my seeds and plants need to grow and thrive. Over the years, I've developed gardening skills, so I've learned to prepare the soil and nurture the environment before planting any seeds.

Similarly, a fulfilling life requires that we prepare for the future by building a strong foundation for our personal and professional growth. The PLANT process begins with understanding ourselves and learning about our values. Fertile ground means creating situations that prepare and provide opportunities for growth and transformation. In this chapter, we are going to explore our values and understand how our values affect and influence our behaviors. Understanding our values is the first step toward creating a more bountiful life. As military spouses, we can prepare and position ourselves for opportunities that allow us to bear fruit and experience abundance within the context of the military community's transitory nature.

I've had a great deal of practice in preparing new garden beds. During our 15-year marriage, my husband and I have moved six times. We moved from California to Montgomery, Alabama. Then we received orders to Washington, D.C., where mid-trip we were diverted to Colorado Springs. From Colorado Springs, we moved to Washington, D.C., and on to Germany, and now we are in Washington, D.C. We are anticipating orders as I write these words. Like most military families, we live our lives on the move. We say home is where the Air Force sends us. Most of my friends, who are married to soldiers and Marines, have moved more frequently. The transient nature of military life is challenging as we work to feel settled, pursue goals, and achieve the desired outcomes we have for our lives. I've often felt uprooted more than I've felt planted.

Every time my husband calls me to say, " Babe, we got new orders today," my initial reaction is sadness because I know a series of goodbyes will quickly follow. There will be goodbyes to my co-workers and friends, tearful goodbyes to my sorority sisters and church community, and goodbyes to my favorite coffee cafes. My second reaction is fear and uncertainty. Like other military spouses, I worry about maintaining career progression and finding a new job. I worry about how my family will adjust to a new community and new schools. Then, I become overwhelmed by the logistics of packing, sorting, and all the details of our move that will not be managed, financially covered, or facilitated by the Department of Defense.

Initially, an emotional swirl takes over my thoughts. The obvious solution to addressing and ending the sense of upheaval I experienced with each move was to begin to proactively plan and prepare for the transient nature of our military lifestyle. We've come to rely on moving preparation checklists. I know that my extensive network of military spouses will help me learn about communities, churches, and the best boutiques.

Whenever we make a permanent change of station (PCS) move, my husband tells the realtor that we will only consider homes with space for a garden. It's one of my essential requirements; it's a "must-have" in my life. I'm willing to pack my entire life in cardboard boxes every two to three years. In exchange, I want space to garden. The reality of our military lifestyle is that we frequently move before the garden has time to mature and fully bloom. My friends ask me, "why do I always plant gardens at the homes we rent for our family?" The answer lies in my values and what I consider most important in my life.

Must Haves and Peak Moments

During our PCS preparation process, my husband and I sit down and list our "must-haves" versus "nice-to-haves" for our housing and community. Our must-haves are the essential things we want in our new home or community to feel safe, comfortable, secure, satisfied, and fulfilled. Our "nice-to-haves" are all the extra, non-essential things, like a wood-burning fireplace and the outdoor kitchen and barbeque space.

When we were purchasing our home, some of our must-haves included a fenced back-yard for our black labradors, four bedrooms, a man-cave, and garden space.

When I thought about it, our must-haves reflected things of particular importance to our overall quality of life. Security and entertaining space, family, and creative expression represent some of my "must-have" items.

During my husband's deployments or TDYs (Temporary Duty) away from home, our dogs provide companionship and security for me. We are often stationed in locations where we don't have family or relatives nearby, so when possible, we want space for extended visits and family gatherings.

Whether or not we are fully aware of our values, they influence our decisions and behaviors. For example, I value creativity, which is encompassed in my decision and enjoyment as an entrepreneur, author, baker and gardener. These activities also embody the high value I place on innovation. When we align our values with our actions, we tend to be more content in our personal and professional lives.

At one point, early in my career, I was struggling to maintain relationships at work. While I believed in the organization's mission, and I was able to utilize my marketing and communications skills, I was often unhappy and frustrated at the end of the working day. During a board meeting, the CEO discussed the volume of work I had produced on a project and referred to me as a "workhorse." While it was an unfortunate choice of words, it nevertheless came to reflect how I felt in that working environment. Even though I met and exceeded my performance targets, I was unhappy and unsatisfied at work. I was not thriving or succeeding within the organizational culture. I began to work with mentors and coaches, who helped me understand how that particular working environment and culture was inconsistent with many of my personal and professional values.

While meeting with my mentor, I remember telling her how frustrating this environment was for me. I was complaining. Okay, I was ranting. In response, she said, "Tell me about a time when you were satisfied or enjoyed a work project. Tell me what you were doing and what made the experience special or fun." Two instances immediately came to mind: One, when I was part of a team working on the Air Force Space Command's Quality of Life and Airmen Resiliency program. The second is whenever I'm digging in the dirt in my garden.

At first glance, these seem to be two divergent activities. But I began to describe these experiences in very similar terms and paradigms. For example, I had the opportunity to learn new things. I was able to put my skills and capabilities to use. Our success required innovation and creativity. Our team had several talented individual contributors who worked through consensus. Our collaborative approach led to new policies and programs that impacted our service members and families. Additionally, we took the time to celebrate our individual and collective accomplishments throughout the project.

This simple discussion planted a critical seed that led me to launch my marketing and communications consultancy a few months later. I wanted to create an environment where my values and talents as a marketing and communications professional, woman of color, and military spouse could be fully engaged. Over the next few months, I began a deliberate process to understand my values, leadership skills, and business acumen so I could become an entrepreneur. Essentially, I started the process to PLANT in my own life. My first step was to prepare by understanding of my environment and myself. I began to prepare my soil to grow into my purpose by working with a leadership coach, reading books, and taking online courses about entrepreneurship and values-driven leadership in particular. If you want to pursue your education, turn your favorite craft into an entrepreneurial enterprise, or live your purpose and experience growth opportunities, I recommend your first step should include determining and understanding your values.

Over time, I've learned that the experiences I described to my mentor are considered peak moments or "moments of highest happiness and fulfillment".[1] Seriously, who doesn't want a life filled with moments of the highest happiness and fulfillment? Usually, these experiences occur when our values align with our actions.

I believe one's values are important because they impact how we structure our lives and guide our priorities. Values are our guiding compass; they help direct and guide our choices, decisions, and plans for ourselves. Our values are the foundation upon which we build our lives and goals. "The decisions we make are a reflection of our values and beliefs, and they direct towards a specific purpose." [2] When we know, honor, and live by our values, life is more purposeful, rewarding, and fulfilling.

I recently asked my 78-year-old mother why she and my father took me to volunteer at a local homeless shelter and kitchen on Saturdays. She said they wanted to teach me the importance of service, compassion, and generosity. As an adult, I've had to determine what I value. Many of the values my parents instilled in me still guide my behaviors and actions. Today, regardless of our duty stations, I still manage to serve and volunteer with community groups.

....

[1] *Privette, G.(2001). Defining moments of self-actualization: Peak performance and peak experience, in K. J. Schneider, J. F. T. Bugental, and J. F. Pierson (Eds.). The Handbook of Humanistic Psychology, 161-180.*

[2] *Barrett, R. (2018). Everything I have learned about values. Lulu Publishing Services.*

There's a lot written on values and the benefits of knowing your values. Life is more manageable and rewarding when we are aware of our values and use them to guide our actions and decisions. As an Air Force officer, my husband relies on the Air Force core values to guide his profession of arms, operations, and decision-making processes. Our values can be used to guide our actions, behaviors, and fulfill us with purpose. If we are living a life that aligns with our values, we tend to grow. We are also more content because we are engaging our time and talents in activities that fulfill us and bring us joy.[3]

Benefits of Knowing our Values

Now, consider some benefits to knowing your values:

1. **Values help identify your purpose.**
   I think we tend to make finding our purpose a big scary, cumbersome boulder in our lives. We tend to view determining how we want to spend our time as a life quest. If we spend some time learning what is important to us and doing those things, we will also find our purpose.

2. **Values help you make difficult or challenging decisions.**
   Remember, values are the guideposts or the compass we use to make decisions or determine our actions. Since values represent foundational beliefs and what is essential in our lives, we can leverage them to make difficult, challenging, and unpopular decisions. Relying and acting consistently with our values can help alleviate the stress and anxiety from decision-making.

....

[3] *Barrett 2018.*

8

3. **Values help improve and build confidence.**

   Knowing our values enables us to form decisions and opinions about subjects and behaviors that are important. To grow and mature, we have to understand our values and beliefs. When we know what is important to us, it doesn't matter what's important to others. The result of acting on our beliefs builds our confidence.

4. **Values help increase our sense of happiness and contentment.**

   If you know your values and engage them purposefully, you can make challenging decisions, improve our confidence and goal attainment. You can also possibly enhance your sense of happiness and contentment. [4]

While values tend to be stable over time, some of our values will change as we mature and as our circumstances change. Understanding our values requires that we pay attention to them over time.

Before we go any further, I want to encourage you to complete the first Stepping Stone activity, which will help you identify and understand your values.

---

[4] *Seligman, M. E. P. (2004). Authentic happiness: Using the new positive psychology to realize your potential for lasting fulfillment (Reprint ed.). Atria Books.*

Here are 5 of my core values:

Creativity • Spirituality • Independence • Achievement • Concern for Others

TapRoot © has developed four steps that are useful in identifying core values:

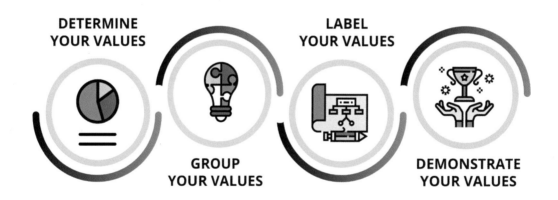

Let's look at each step more closely:

1. **Determine your Values**

   From the list below, choose every core value that has significant meaning to you. Try not to overthink your selection. As you scan through the list, circle or underline the words that reflect your core values.

VALUES LIST			
Abundance	Daring	Intuition	Preparedness
Acceptance	Decisiveness	Joy	Proactivity
Accountability	Dedication	Kindness	Professionalism
Achievement	Dependability	Knowledge	Punctuality
Advancement	Diversity	Leadership	Recognition
Adventure	Empathy	Learning	Relationships
Advocacy	Encouragement	Love	Reliability
Ambition	Enthusiasm	Loyalty	Resilience
Appreciation	Ethics	Making a Difference	Resourcefulness
Attractivness	Excellence	Mindfulness	Responsibility
Autonomy	Expressiveness	Motivation	Responsiveness
Balance	Fairness	Optimism	Security
Being hte best	Family	Open-Mindedness	Self-Control
Benevolence	Friendships	Originality	Selflessness
Boldness	Flexibility	Passion	Simplicity
Brilliance	Freedom	Performance	Stability
Calmness	Fun	Personal	Success

Caring	Generosity	Development	Teamwork
Challenge	Grace	Proactive	Thankfulness
Charity	Growth	Professionalism	Thoughtfulness
Cheerfulness	Flexibility	Quality	Traditionalism
Cleverness	Happiness	Recognition	Trustworthiness
Community	Health	Risk-Taking	Understanding
Commitment	Honesty	Safety	Uniqueness
Compassion	Humility	Security	Usefulness
Cooperation	Humor	Service	Versatility
Collaboration	Inclusiveness	Spirituality	Vision
Consistency	Independence	Stability	Warmth
Contribution	Individuality	Peace	Wealth
Creativity	Innovation	Perfection	Well-Being
Credibility	Inspiration	Playfulness Popularity	Wisdom
Curiosity	Intelligence	Power	Zeal

VALUES LIST			

2. Group similar values together.

These groupings should be meaningful to you. Try not to create more than five categories. Here's an example.

SAMPLE VALUES GROUPING		
Achievement	Playfulness	Advocacy
Growth	Humor	Community
Innovation	Fun	Making a Difference
Intelligence		Service
Knowledge		
Learning		

Group Your Values (1-5 Groups)				
Values 1	**Values 2**	**Values 3**	**Values 4**	**Values 5**

3. **Select or highlight one word in each grouping that represents all the values in each group.**

   Select what describes the value best for you. I've provided an example below.

VALUES SUMMARY		
Achievement	Playfulness	Advocacy
Growth	Humor	Community
Innovation	Fun	Making a Difference
Intelligence		Service
Knowledge		
Learning		

Write your final list of values in order of importance to you:

_____

_____

_____

_____

_____

_____

_____

4. Demonstrate your Values [5]

Respond to the following questions for each of your values:

- What does this value mean to me?

_____

_____

_____

_____

_____

- How do I act upon or demonstrate this value?

_____

_____

_____

_____

_____

[5] *TapRoot Root Cause Analysis Training, Software, and Consulting. (n.d.). Retrieved September 21, 2020, from http://www.taproot.com/archives/3777.*

Congratulations, you've just identified your core life values. This is the first and critical step in the PLANT process, which will help move you towards achieving your goals and a more fulfilling life. Our values represent the fertile soil that we will use to grow our future.

Now that you have identified your values, try to think of them like seeds. Plant them by putting them into practice in your attitudes and daily actions. Planting a seed is the simple act of setting into motion something that will help you create the life you want. Seeds don't stay seeds forever. Once planted, over time, something new springs up; we see progress and growth. In the way gardeners prepare soil, we need to prepare a strong foundation for our plans and future. The Digging Deeper Reflections will help you integrate your values in your life.

> Allow your newly acquired awareness of your values to guide your decision-making, perceptions, and actions.

Let me share an example of how I've incorporated my values into my company.

MY VALUES - Influencing My Actions & Decisions

Concern for Others
Embodied in my commitment to hiring military spouses and veterans, and our mission to work with military organizations and emerging entrepreneurs

Independence
Reflected in my entrepreneurial business and matrix reporting structure for my teammates and colleagues.

Creativity
Embodied in the marketing, artistic and design mission of my company.

Our values are seeds we can plant to build more abundant lives and experiences. In the next section, we will continue to use the PLANT process to look at how we can use our values to make decisions and take action towards our goals.

"For where your treasure is, there your heart will be also."

Matthew 6:21 (NKJV)

1. Rewrite this scripture in your own words.

_____

_____

_____

_____

_____

_____

_____

_____

_____

_____

2. **Using the journaling space below, write about your "Peak Moments." I've included some questions and writing prompts to get you started.**

    -   Write about 2-3 moments in time when your life or work was full and rewarding.

        _____

        _____

        _____

        _____

        _____

        _____

        _____

    -   What were you doing?

        _____

        _____

        _____

        _____

        _____

        _____

        _____

- What about this moment stands out for you?

_____

_____

_____

_____

_____

_____

_____

- What do you remember about the environment?

_____

_____

_____

_____

_____

_____

_____

- What need or desire was met?

_____

_____

_____

_____

_____

_____

- Why was the moment meaningful?

_____

_____

_____

_____

_____

- What other things made this moment important to you?

_____

_____

_____

- How were the core values you've identified represented in that moment?

_____

_____

_____

_____

_____

_____

_____

- Write three ways you can incorporate your values in your life through your actions and decisions.

_____

_____

_____

_____

_____

_____

Additional Resources

The Life Values Inventory©, a free values clarification assessment and online tool which helps to clarify values and serves as a blueprint for decision-making and life planning. [6] Completing the assessment takes about 5 to 7 minutes. You will receive a summary of your top 15 values. You can also categorize your values in order of importance.

Go to: **https://my.lifevaluesinventory.org/account/create** to take the survey.

---

[6] *Crace, R. Kelly, Ph.D. and Brown, Duane. (1996) LifeValues Inventory Applied Psychology Resources, Inc.*

LEVERAGE

*"A wise man will hear and increase learning, and a
man of understanding will attain wise counsel."*
Proverbs 1:5 (NKJV)

Sometimes, in the middle of a project or a specific gardening task, I find that I need thick gloves to protect my hands, or a wider shovel to dig a deep hole. As we discussed in the previous chapter, I need the right mix of soil, compost, and fertilizer to ensure my plants thrive. Nothing is more frustrating than growing blue hydrangeas when you want pink ones! The amount of pH in the soil affects the color and vitality of the hydrangea blossoms. It seems obvious, but planting a garden requires that you have the right environment, tools, and resources to stimulate plant growth.

The second step of the PLANT process involves leveraging our values, engaging core strengths, and accessing resources and relationships to achieve desired outcomes and goals. Leverage means that we will use our values, core strengths, and other available resources within our community to gain additional opportunities and resources.

Gardeners rely on the U.S. Department of Agriculture Plant Hardiness Zone Map to provide a standard guide of conditions relevant to plant growth and survival. The zones define what plants grow best in some regions of the country. Planting zones are an easy way to understand when to plant. Some vegetables can be planted before the last frost; some cannot. It's the number of growing days that dictates what and when you can plant. Guess what, here's a little secret--any vegetable will grow where you live. Everyone in the contiguous United States lives in Zone 3 or higher and has at least a 123-day growing season - enough to produce any vegetable, including watermelons, pumpkins and butternut squash.[7] The key is knowing when and how to plant for a plentiful harvest. Many vegetables don't tolerate frost and have to be planted after the last frost date. Planting too soon will often result in limp, frostbitten vegetables.

Similarly, regardless of where we are stationed, we can plant our goals and live abundant lives. But, we have to ensure the conditions and circumstances are conducive to the growth and development of our plans. There are several resources and relationships within the military community that can be leveraged and engaged in creating advantageous conditions for our future goals and ambitions.

....

[7] *https://planthardiness.ars.usda.gov/PHZMWeb/*

Understanding the Environment

When I first started my company, in my mind, it was a global Fortune 500 conglomerate, not a one-woman shop operating in the dining room. While I had the desire and intent to start my own communications consultancy, I lacked the practical knowledge to launch and manage a business on my own. I didn't know if I needed to incorporate or be a sole proprietorship. More importantly, I didn't understand the tax laws and tax implications for our family, which caused more than a ripple in our annual tax bill during my first year of operations. After paying an additional $10,000 in federal income taxes, it was abundantly apparent that I had launched my firm before I understood the business operating requirements and environment to ensure my company, my savings, and our marriage would last. I had a great deal to learn about launching and running a consultancy.

Given the vast resources currently available throughout the U.S. in local communities and on global military installations through the Readiness, Education, and Family Support centers, substantial opportunities exist for spouses to pursue their personal, educational, and professional goals. In many ways, the environment for military spouses to access additional opportunities is rapidly evolving and expanding. Just as plants can grow in any geographic location, we can grow and thrive regardless of our duty stations. Leveraging these resources created additional opportunities and relationships that helped solidify the viability of my company.

A trip to the Airmen and Family Readiness Center on base opened the door to a treasure trove of support and resources. Through programs offered by the Small Business Administration (SBA) and Syracuse University's Institute for Veterans and Military Families (IVMF), I learned business management and entrepreneurial requirements. I received mentoring in the fundamentals of business ownership, small business resources, and networking to launch my consultancy successfully. I leveraged others' expertise, talent, skills, and resources to create a more conducive environment for my business.

In the evenings and on weekends, I attended in-person and online workshops with business professionals who helped me write a business plan, build my confidence, and expand my knowledge bases. I met other entrepreneurs who became my mentors, role models, and in some cases, my clients and business partners. During my second year of operations, I was earning a six-figure salary. I had to hire three independent contractors to help provide marketing services for a portfolio of clients across the U.S. Now, I'm once again working with V-WISE to develop a growth and diversification plan for my company. The attorney, tax consultant, and financial advisor I met at the local SBA Women's Business and Incubator Center continue to provide professional services to my consultancy. Once I understood the business-operating requirements, I could leverage my knowledge to develop plans to manage and grow my business effectively.

The PLANT process focuses on leveraging as a way to develop the relationships and access resources we need to manage complex and complicated processes, manage unstable environments, and build reliable networks. By leveraging resources and relations, we can garner the support we need to plant, grow, and transform our delayed or stalled desires and dreams into achievable plans.

Using Our Strengths

In the previous chapter, we spent time identifying and understanding our values. In this section, we will learn about and determine our character strengths so we can leverage them with our values to develop action plans to achieve our goals.

I'm talking about learning, engaging, and leveraging the unique character strengths that we have to achieve our purpose.[8] The PLANT process empowers us to leverage our values and strengths, creating environments that nurture and allow for our continuous growth.

I was diagnosed with breast cancer at age 35. At the time, I was single and had relocated to a city where I didn't have any family and or friends. I could feel a lump in my right breast. It was painful and hard. I went to 4 different physicians in two different states before one took my concern seriously and ordered a mammogram. As it turned out, those test results were misdiagnosed as dense breast tissue.

The persistent pain in my right breast caused me to schedule an appointment with another breast specialist, who immediately scheduled another mammogram and needle biopsy. After months of fighting for a physician to take my medical concern seriously, everything began to unravel quickly after this appointment. I didn't have time to wait for my mother to come to town before my surgery. So, my mom took a cab from the airport to pick me up at the hospital. I was so confident that the needle biopsy would be clear, that I sent my mom back home three days later, and I returned to work. Two days later, when I met with my doctor he wouldn't look at me. He was looking at my chart, not at me. Immediately, my heart started racing. He said, "You have breast cancer. You need to have a mastectomy as soon as possible. Given your age, race, and how aggressive your cancer is, I suggest you have a bi-lateral mastectomy immediately. We can get you in within the next two weeks. I know a good plastic surgeon that will fix you back up". My ears started ringing. He handed me the lab report that had "Estrogen Receptor-Positive" highlighted in yellow. Then, he said,

....

[8] Peterson, C., & Seligman, M. (2004). *Character strengths and virtues: A handbook and classification (1st ed.).* American Psychological Association; Oxford University Press.

go home and rest. My nurse will call you with additional information and a referral to an oncologist". I thought, I'm 35, I ran 5 miles this morning, and I don't have children. I said to him, "I can't have cancer. I'm just getting started in life". Now, he looked directly in my eyes, and he responded, "Eugenia, you have cancer, and it is aggressive." And he left the room.

Cancer is insidious; like darkness, it sneaks up on you, causing you to stumble and feel unbalanced and vulnerable. It choked me. It took my breath away, making me disoriented and dizzy. I felt the room spinning, spinning, and spiraling. Then, I heard a ringing in my ears. My chest was tight. My breathing, was I still breathing? That's how I always feel when I step back to that moment in my mind. I know on the way to the parking lot, I rested my hand and head on the office building's brick wall. I thought I would fall or throw up.

I don't remember calling my mother. I don't know what I said. I don't know if I cried. All I remember was feeling dizzy. I know I called my mother because my sister kept calling me back, but I didn't pick up the phone because I couldn't talk.

I was frightened at the prospect of having breast surgery, reconstruction, and months of chemotherapy. I had to figure out these medical terms and the medications they wanted me to take. I was faced with a barrage of medical appointments. I was worried about how I would be able to work because I needed health insurance, the means to pay my mortgage and my student loans. If I were able to conceive a child after my chemo treatments, I surely would not be able to breastfeed. Over the next several days, I mourned the husband, the children, the life that I believed I would no longer have.

We've sexualized breasts. Big voluptuous breasts are everywhere. But, let me tell you, there is nothing sexy about breast cancer. Scars the width of your chest are not sexy. Vomiting is not sexy. There is nothing sexy about chemo treatments turning your lips, tongue, fingers, and toes black. Losing my hair was traumatic and transformational.

African American women are always thinking about our hair. We are raised knowing that our hair is our crown of glory. My hair began falling out after my first chemo treatment. For me, it was emotionally and physically painful. First, it was just a few strands here and there when I combed my hair in the morning. Then, one morning when I removed my hair scarf, my hair came out in my hands. By day five or seven, I was losing clumps of my hair. I cried and cried and cried. Standing in the mirror, I was horrified at what looked back at me. Later that week, my hairstylist opened the salon early so she could shave off my hair. The only sound in her salon was the buzz of the clippers and frequent sniffles. I was supposed to attend a briefing at Arizona State University later in the morning. As we were finishing my hair cut, my manager called to make sure I would attend. A few moments later, one of the administrators from the university called, too. No one knew that I was at the salon that morning.

I wanted to go home, crawl under the covers and let this disease consume me. Instead, I put on my navy blue business suit and pearls. I arrived on time, bald, and wearing red lipstick.

I felt small. I wanted to disappear. I wore red lipstick thinking it would distract everyone from my baldness. Standing in the center of the room, with all eyes focused on me, for the first time in the process, I was surrounded by love, laughter, and joy. At my most vulnerable moment, others saw defiance and bravery. I liked the Eugenia that I saw, reflecting in their eyes. Later that night, I prayed and asked God to help me be that Eugenia.

I worked during my treatments. Every three weeks, I received a three-hour treatment. While I had compassionate and exceptional care, the process for me was dreadful. After every treatment, I got sicker and sicker and weaker and weaker. My mom and I could predict when the vomiting would start, down to the hour. Within 48-hours of my chemo cocktail, I was going to vomit for the next 2 to 3 days. The anti-nausea medications did not work for me. For my mom and the oncology team, it was a constant battle to keep me hydrated and nourished. My 5-mile runs became daily walks to the corner of my block. I met my neighbors because when I couldn't catch my breath, I would sit on their front stoops.

My nurse introduced me to other women in treatment, and I found my way into Arizona's wellness community. Of course, these women were 20 and 30 years older than I was at the time. But with grace, they taught me how to submit to the process, but not to the disease. I began to gather information about breast cancer and my treatment protocol.

Once I reached the halfway point in my treatment protocol, my friends celebrated my milestone with a crazy hat party that raised $6,000 for our local cancer wellness center. My oncologist, who always looked me in the eye, told me that all indicators showed that the treatment was working. I started to workout with a cancer rehab therapist at the local YMCA. She handed me a Campbell's soup can on our weightlifting day, which became too heavy for me after five reps. But over time, I progressed to a 3-pound weight, to a 5-pound weight, and eventually a 15-pound weight. Now, I think about the times when I couldn't lift my arms at all, and I feel grateful.

I've been in remission for 20 years. I've negotiated peace with the scars on my chest. Cancer taught and helped me find my strengths. We are stronger than we know because our values and inherent character strengths guide us and help us navigate circumstances and situations. Cancer taught me that I am more resilient and stronger than I would have believed. Although I didn't realize it at the time, my values and core character strengths engaged in helping me manage my cancer diagnosis and treatment protocol. The PLANT process encourages us to understand our values and character strengths so we can lever-age them to create environments and experiences that nurture and cultivate the garden of our lives.

Knowing your Strengths

Everyone has character strengths that we can tap into to navigate situations, achieve our goals, and improve our fulfillment.[9] Using and engaging our character strengths allows us to create lives that are full and rewarding. Knowing and using our strengths also builds and reinforces our resilience, allowing us to manage the demands of our military lifestyles and the routines of life.

Character strengths are simply traits that everyone has and uses to varying degrees. Some people easily express gratitude or forgiveness; others show bravery and courage more readily. Researchers and psychologists have identified 24 character strengths that can be classified into six categories.[10] See Appendix II to review the 24 character strengths.

The Six Character Strengths Categories			
	Wisdom & Knowledge (creativity, curiosity, open-mindedness, love of learning, perspective)		**Justice** (citizenship, fairness, leadership)
	Courage (bravery, persistence, integrity, vitality)		**Temperance** (forgiveness, humility, prudence, self-regulation)
	Humanity (love, kindness, social intelligence)		**Transcendence** (beauty/excellence, gratitude, hope, humor, spirituality)(11)

[9] Peterson, C., & Seligman, M. (2004).

[10] Peterson, C., & Seligman, M. (2004).

During Operation Iraqi Freedom and Operation Enduring Freedom, researchers from the University of Pennsylvania worked with the Department of Defense to help service members use their character strengths to build and sustain resiliency.[11] These studies provided valuable insights that informed the wellness and resiliency programs of all six-service branches.

Whether someone is active duty, a military spouse, or a civilian, the same general principles can be applied. We all have some core and dominant character strengths. Knowing and using our character strengths can help with our resilience and lead us toward more meaningful lives.[12]

Once I understood my character strengths, I began to shift my behaviors and perspectives to use and accentuate my character strengths and values. I started to make decisions and take actions that reinforced my values and strengths. I reduced my stress and began to build more rewarding and enjoyable life experiences. The PLANT process enables us to leverage our values, core strengths, available resources, and relationships to create new opportunities and provide stability for developing and launching our future plans.

[11] Peterson, C., & Seligman, M. (2004).

[12] Peterson, C., & Seligman, M. (2004).

STEPPING STONE *Activities*

The studies I mentioned above also led to the development of the VIA (Values in Action) Character Strengths Survey; it's a free online survey that identifies and summarizes character strengths. More than 8 million people around the world have taken the VIA.[13]

Take the VIA Character Strengths Survey online at **https://www.viacharacter.org/survey/account/register.**

All you have to do is register using an email address and create a password. Once you complete the survey, you will receive a detailed summary of your character strengths. If you select to receive emails from the VIA Character Institute, you will receive emails with exercises, information, and resources to help you continue to understand and leverage your character strengths.

Write you character strengths here:

_____

_____

_____

_____

....

[13] Peterson, C., & Seligman, M. (2004).

Write your values here:

_____

_____

_____

_____

_____

_____

_____

_____

_____

_____

_____

_____

_____

_____

_____

Character Strengths Summary			
Character Strength	Summary Meaning	How can I use this Strength	

	Based on the VIA Character Survey, my signature strengths are:	
	Spirituality **(Transcendence)**	
	Creativity **(Wisdom)**	
	Perseverance **(Courage)**	
	Love of Learning **(Wisdom)**	
	Honesty **(Courage)**	

EXAMPLE

CREATIVITY

SPIRITUALITY

ACHIEVEMENT

INDEPENDICE

CONCERN FOR OTHERS

MY VALUES ARE:

After filling many journals and working with professional leadership coaches, I understand that my values and character strengths related to perseverance and courage helped me navigate my cancer diagnosis, treatment, and recovery. My spirituality helped ground and sustain me during my breast cancer. Recently, I was diagnosed with a rare condition called smoldering multiple myeloma, a rare blood cancer. Rather than worry and feel anxiety, I'm choosing to approach this medical diagnosis using my faith, allowing me to engage and leverage my core strengths and values directly.

The changes and challenges resulting from our military moves, restarting my career, and launching my consultancy are more natural for me to manage because I've learned to engage my strengths, align my actions with my values, and leverage resources and relationships available to me. There's no magic bullet or secret keycard to unlocking building our resiliency and achieving fulfillment. If I can leverage my values and character strengths to PLANT and overcome challenges and accomplish my goals and experience fulfillment, so can you.

"For God has not given us a spirit of fear, but of power and love and of a sound mind."

2 Timothy 1:7 (NKJV)

1. **Rewrite this scripture in your own words.**
   Think back to a particular moment in time when you had to overcome an obstacle or a challenge.

_____

_____

_____

_____

_____

_____

_____

_____

- Write a summary of that experience.

_____

_____

_____

_____

_____

_____

_____

- What did you have to do to overcome this challenge or situation?

_____

_____

_____

_____

_____

_____

- What did you learn from this experience?

_____

_____

_____

_____

_____

_____

_____

- Considering your VIA Character Traits Survey, what strengths do you think you used in this situation?

_____

_____

_____

_____

_____

_____

_____

_____

- What can you do to make sure you engage your character strengths over the next week?

_____

_____

_____

_____

_____

_____

_____

_____

_____

_____

_____

_____

_____

ACTION

"For I know the plans that I have for you, declares the Lord, "plans to prosper you and not to harm you, plans to give you hope and a future."
Jeremiah 29:11 (NKJV)

In 2011, we received short notice orders, so we selected our new rental online. Yep, that's right. We didn't have the time to travel to our new duty station for a house-hunting trip. So, we did what was efficient. We used the website, Military By Owner, selected a house that met our essential needs, and we wired the required deposit. Two days later, after driving from Colorado Springs to Northern Virginia, I felt myself frown when we pulled into the driveway of our new townhome. At first sight, the weeds, overgrowth, and disorder of the garden beds were discouraging and underwhelming. Realizing I had a blank canvas, I became excited.

I had an opportunity to engage, create, and to develop something new. As I began another job search and unpacked our household goods, my mind would wander to colorful daylilies, hydrangeas, poppies, and azaleas. During the day, I began to pay attention to how the sun appeared and disappeared along the fence line and entryway to the house. Once the cable guy showed up, I used Google and Pinterest to gather information and inspiration on what to plant around the house. I began to consider which flowers and garden spaces would make lovely hideaways and entertaining spaces for new friends and our family when they came to visit. I used these images of flowers and landscape designs to inspire and create my vision for the garden. My ideas would guide the actions I could take to plan and create flourishing, vibrant garden beds.

When you plant a garden, you have to create a landscaping plan. Similarly, a good life plan will produce a bountiful life. Using the PLANT process, we are at the point where we are ready for Action. This chapter has two sections. In the first section, we will use our values, strengths, and goals to develop an action board. Then, we will convert our action boards into a MAP (My Action Plan).

From Vision to Action

Every year, usually in December or January, my friends and I get together for a girls retreat. At some point over the weekend, we will spend an afternoon or evening creating action boards representing our plans for the coming year. We grab our old magazines, poster boards, construction paper, glitter, scissors, and glue sticks. We prepare our creative space with candles, music, incense, wine, and a lot of food and desserts. We each state our intention for the year, because resolutions are too stressful. Then, we individually find our space and create our boards for the year.

Over the next few weeks, I convert my action board into an action plan. I put my yearly goals and hopes into action by creating mini-action plans. Planning helps me organize and take steps towards the goals on my action board.

I hang my boards in my home office. I take a photo of my board, so I always have it on my cell phone. On a few occasions, I've shared them on my social media platforms. I pray over them, and at least once a week, I devote time to updating my board to ensure I stay focused and accountable.

You're probably familiar with vision boards, which focus on using pictures and words to represent your hopes, dreams, and desires. Vision boards use a creative process to set clear intentions and goals for what you want to manifest in your life.[14] The ideology behind vision boards is that by focusing on your dreams and hopes, you can attract or manifest them.[15] Vision boards draw on the "Law of Attraction" that you've heard so much about in the mass media.

I believe we have to do more than visualize our futures and hopes. No matter your goal, you're going to have to take some action to achieve it. PLANT Process helps us take steps towards achieving our goals. So, rather than discussing vision boards, let's focus on action boards and their importance in goal setting and making a bountiful life garden.

In the book, Throw Your Vision Board Away, Neil Farber argues that, "We need more than a vision to change or improve things, we need an action board."[16] An action board engages your vision, values, core strengths, accountability, and goal setting to help achieve and accomplish goals.[17] Developing an action board involves adding measurable goals and dates to your vision; it provides a framework for achieving goals.

The next Stepping Stone activity involves using our values, strengths, and interests to create an action board.

[14] Losier, M. J. (2020). Law of attraction The science of attracting more of what you want and less of what you don't [2006] (2nd ed.). Michael J. Losier.

[15] Losier, M. J. (2020).

[16] Farber, Neil E. (2016). Throw your vision board away: The truth about the Law of Attraction. CreateSpace Independent Publishing Platform.

[17] Farber, Neil E. (2016).

1. **Gather your supplies**

   In general, you will need the following supplies:

   - something to attach images to, such as:

     ° blank art book with mixed media paper

     ° poster board

     ° a large sheet of paper

     ° a corkboard

     ° glue, clips, or pins

     ° markers, pens, paint

     ° colorful or plain paper for adding personal flair

     ° Magazines and books for photos, images, and words.

2. **Create a Special Space and Time to Work**

   As you begin this part of the activity, take some time to create a calm and creative environment. Play some music, light a few candles, or maybe sit in the park. The point is to get yourself into a space where you can connect with yourself, your ideas and your goals.

3. Identify your Goals

Make a list of goals you'd like to achieve in the next year. Consider some categories like social goals, professional goals, physical goals, and spiritual goals as guides to help you get started. Sometimes, I add a family category too. Other times, I've developed an action board that focuses on one specific action, like starting my own company or planning, completing my doctoral studies, or writing a book. The intent at this point is just to begin identifying the area or areas that you want to include in your action plan.

What's important is that you think about 3-5 goals important to you. Here's an example of the four areas I used for one of the action boards.

Personal:	Say no to people, projects, and activities that do not bring me joy or fulfillment.
Social:	Expand CommunisPR portfolio with 15 new clients during 2020 Participate in GOTV Festival Plan monthly dinner date with El
Physical:	Practice yoga at least 3x a week beginning in Jan Walk 30 minutes a day after work daily Reduce working hours to 9 hours a day and do not work on Saturdays Complete 100 hours of yoga instructor training before December 2020
Spiritual:	Participate in three Proverbs 31 online bible study sessions during 2020 Begin and end each day in prayer Learn to meditate using the Chopra Center 21-day meditation app

Action Board Focus Areas

Personal • Social • Spiritual • Physical • Profession

4. **Create Your Action Board**

   Set aside a few hours while the children are at school, one weekend, or over a few evenings to select pictures, images or sayings that represent your goals and inspire you. Select words that reflect the goals you want to achieve in the next 12 to 18 months.

   For example, I want to complete my professional yoga instructor training by April 2021. So my board includes yoga images and the words April 2021.

   Your action board uses images, photographs, quotes, and sayings that represent your goals, not your feelings or dreams. Try to incorporate your values and strengths in your action board too.

5. **Display your Action Board**

   Well done! Now, hang your board in your home, work, and take a photo with your cell phone. Displaying the action board helps you continually focus on your goals. On more than a few occasions, I placed items from my action board on my annual performance plan. I worked at Intel Corporation while I was writing my dissertation. I told my manager about the action board I created. He suggested I include completing my dissertation in my annual performance plan. Score! Not only was I able to achieve my goal, I earned a bonus for completing my dissertation that summer.

"I know the plans that I have for you, declares the Lord, plans to prosper you and not to harm you, plans to give you hope and a future."

Jeremiah 29:11 (NKJV)

- Considering your action board, can you rewrite this scripture in your own words.

_____

_____

_____

_____

- What common themes do you see on your action board?

_____

_____

_____

_____

54

- How do these goals align with your strengths and values?

_____

_____

_____

_____

_____

_____

_____

- What surprises you about your action board?

_____

_____

_____

_____

_____

_____

- What do your current actions tell you about your vision for your future?

_____

_____

_____

_____

_____

_____

_____

- What do you have to change to achieve the goals or plans in your action board?

_____

_____

_____

_____

_____

_____

MAP the Way Ahead

I began writing this book while creating a new garden after our PCS to Germany. My new home was 4,013 miles away from my childhood home. I was struggling to learn a new language so that I could function in our host country. I wanted to learn the language so I could participate more fully in the local culture and grocery shop on the economy. I failed my German driving test twice. Once I got my driver's license, I ended up getting lost every time I left the house because the Exchange had sold out of GPS systems. Still, I was anxious to explore. I began to view my lost treks as adventures, just like my wandering on the paths and wooded trails. I had to step far outside of my comfort zone to meet new people and find my way around.

We lived in a lovely community 20 minutes from the military installation near Stuttgart, Germany. Most of the families in our neighborhood spent substantial time growing fruits and vegetables for their families. My grandmother and mother taught me how to grow herbs and flowers. I grew up in the city, and like most folks, I purchased my tomatoes, zucchini, and cucumbers from the neighborhood grocery store. I knew little to nothing about growing food to sustain my family until I moved to Germany. As luck would have it, my neighbors were anxious to help me embrace this aspect of the German culture. In addition to helping me learn German, my neighbors were more than willing to help me plant a vegetable garden. My neighbors shared seedlings with me. They even drew me a map to the neighborhood nursery. In return, I taught them how to make authentic buffalo wings and my great grandmother's sweet potato pie.

Unfortunately, the only sunny spot in our yard was on top of the garage and, of course, it was weed infested. Once again, I would have to haul soil, compost, and hoses to build my garden plots. The enormity of all this work was overwhelming. I felt stuck in the weeds. I had the desire to grow organic vegetables for my family, but I didn't know how or where to begin. If I was going to achieve my goal and get out of the weeds, I needed an action plan. If there is one thing that I am sure of, God never gives us a goal or dream without also providing us with a way to achieve it. All I need is a MAP or My Action Plan.

MAP: My Action Plan

It's helpful to think of an action plan like a map. Our GPS apps provide guidance; they map the course ahead to our desired destinations. The action board you recently created encompasses your goals and will help you create a My Action Plan (MAP). The MAP identifies and details all the tasks and steps needed to accomplish goals. Your action board contains goals and what you plan for your future. The MAP includes timelines and milestones that help break down the primary goals into smaller, more manageable steps that propel us closer to achieving our goals and outcomes A MAP enables you to reach your target efficiently by assigning a timeframe to every step. Also, a MAP can make it easier for you to monitor progress and keep your projects on schedule.

Here's a quick example of the action plan I used to create my vegetable garden in Germany.

My goal was to prepare two 2'X4' raised garden beds to harvest organic herbs and vegetables for cooking during summer and fall 2019.

GARDEN MAP			
Month	Acvtivity	Month	Activity
January	Research and determine the types of herbs and planting conditions. Determine the budget for equipment and maintenance, soil, fertilizer, and herbs I want to plant.	April 1st	Remove weeds
February 1st	Purchase seeds and soil and other materials	April 15th	Build and install raised garden boxes. Lay protective overlay. Begin to prepare soil.
Feburary 28th	Start vegetable seeds using grow lights in the basement (Milestone Goal)	May 20th **Milestone Goal**	After the last frost, plant starter vegetables in the garden box. (Milestone Goal)
March 15th	Purchase and assemble raised garden bed. Order compost and soil.	May - June	Monitor for bugs and disease. Maintain plants.
June - October (Goal Accomplished)		Harvest vegetables(Goal Accomplished)	

This stepping stone activity will help you develop a MAP for achieving the goals you've identified on your action board. There are five steps to creating a MAP.

- **Set Goals**

- **Determine Essential Action**

- **Establish Timeline and Milestones**

- **Identify Resources**

- **Monitor Progress and Make Adjustments**

1. **Set Goals**

   Try to write goals that are clear and well defined and directly related to your desired outcome. Make sure your goals can be measured, allowing you to track your progress and results. Also, set milestones and completion dates to ensure you make timely progress towards achieving your goals.

2. **Determine Essential Action**

   Now that you've determined your goal, use the Task Worksheet to break down the steps you need to take to achieve the stated objective. Make sure each task is attainable. Remember, if you have a complicated task, break it down into smaller and smaller steps until it becomes easier to manage.

3. **Develop Timelines & Milestones**

   Next, create a timeline in conjunction with your goals, by prioritizing the steps and, in some cases, the sub-steps. Begin adding schedules or deadlines before you progress to the next levels. Milestones are the mini-goals or short-term goals that you accomplish while working towards your final goal or objective. Achieving milestones is an excellent way to stay motivated, especially if you are working on a multi-year goal.

[Diagram 3] Backward Goal Setting

I use backward goal-setting to develop my milestones and timelines.[18] Diagram 3 summarizes the Backward Goal-setting process, which is used in education settings. The idea is to start with the end goal and then work backward to develop the milestones, tasks, and timelines needed to achieve the final goal.[19] Using this process, I build in milestones or significant tasks that must be accomplished to achieve the goal. Try to think of your milestones as the mile markers you will pass on the way to your final destination. Milestones provide the opportunity to celebrate your progress and accomplishments and allow making any goal adjustments along the way to the final destination.

Look at the rooftop garden MAP example again:

(1) I began with my final goal, what I wanted to achieve by a specific date.

Final Goal:

My goal was to harvest organic vegetables in May-October 2019.

(2) I thought about what milestones and interim steps I needed to take to complete my ultimate goal on time. What did I have to do, and by what date, to achieve my final objective. I continued to work backward, asking what must be done and what resources are needed to achieve the goal.

....

[18] *Goal setting: How to create an action plan and achieve your goals (2nd edition) by Susan B. Wilson and Michael S. Dobson. (2008). Personnel Psychology, 61(4), 931–933.*

[19] *Wiggins, G., and J. McTighe. (1998) Understanding by Design. Merrill Prentice Hall.*

Milestones and Tasks:

Month	Acvtivity	Month	Activity
May 20th Milestone Goal	After the last frost, plant starter vegetables in the garden box. (Milestone Goal)	**April 15th**	Build and install raised garden boxes. Lay protective overlay. Begin to prepare soil.
March 15th	Purchase and assemble raised garden bed. Order compost and soil.	**Feburary 28th**	Start vegetable seeds using grow lights in the basement (Milestone Goal)

(3) If I was going to begin harvesting herbs and vegetables in the summer, I needed to start working on my goal in January. Accomplishing my milestone goals in February and May helped ensure I met my final goal of harvesting vegetables in the summer.

January- Research and determine the types of herbs and planting conditions. Determine the budget for equipment and maintenance, soil, fertilizer, and herbs I want to plant.

4. **Identify Needed Resources**

   As with any project, it's essential to have the resources you need to complete the various tasks. A quick brainstorm session can often help you list out the resources required. Be sure to consider budget, supplies, and people resources if these things are relevant to achieving your goals. When you know what you need to make a project successful, you can efficiently plan out the best way to use them. Identifying and securing the support you need at the start of the project reduces the chances of delays and helps ensure that you make continual progress towards achieving the identified plans and goals.

   Remember, I had to purchase seeds, soil, and other supplies to achieve my goal. These resources were critical and impacted by finances and time management considerations. Without securing resources in advance, I wasn't going to be able to harvest any crops. As you complete the My Action Plan template, consider all the support you will need, including money, supplies, technology, professional expertise, and people.

   Taking the time to consider the things that we want to plant in our lives, and then developing a MAP to achieve or pursue those goals helps us focus on priorities and provides a sense of purpose and assurance.

5. **Monitor and Evaluate**

   In practice, you will continuously monitor and evaluate your progress toward your goal by using the worksheets provided in the Appendix. You should make any mid-course adjustments to ensure your goals remain relevant, achievable and attainable.

   The garden MAP we just used has aspects that incorporate my values and my top character strengths. Spending time gardening engages my creativity, my spirituality, and my love of learning and achievement. I'm able to spend countless hours in the garden because I'm participating in an activity that engages my values and leverages my character strengths, giving me a sense of joy and fulfillment. So, now you are beginning to see how the PLANT process moves you towards your goals and desired outcomes.

I used the PLANT process to create my company, CommunisPR. Once I identified my values and character strengths, I used the resources in my community to develop an action plan to achieve my goal of opening a marketing and communications consultancy. You will notice that my vision board contains references to my business, see the words "a simple plan," "clients," "press," and "communicate." I prepared the foundation for my business by learning about and identifying my values and strengths. I attended courses offered by the Institute for Veterans and Military Families (IVMF) at Syracuse University to learn about entrepreneurship. I used my new knowledge to write my business plan, network and build relationships, and launch my consultancy.

When my husband received orders to Germany, the usual stress ensued. This time, I also had additional concerns about how I would maintain my company's operations. Working with my business mentor and financial consultant, we mapped a strategy that would allow me to continue to operate my U.S. based company, retaining most of my clients while we resided in Germany for three years. As military spouses, we can bloom where we are planted. We just have to put some action alongside our dreams and plans, despite the unforeseen obstacles we may encounter.

Now, develop your MAP. There are extra worksheets in the Appendix.

My Action Plan (MAP) Worksheet

My Values:

_____

_____

_____

_____

_____

_____

My Character Strengths:

_____

_____

_____

_____

_____

_____

My Action Plan		
	Essential Actions	**Milestone & Timelines**
Goal 1		
Goal 2		
	Resources	**Progress**
Goal 1		
Goal 2		

STEPPING STONE *Activities*

*"Write the vision and make it plain on tablets, that he may
run who reads it. For the vision is yet for an appointed time…"*

Habakkuk 2:2-3 (NKJV)

- What does the scripture mean to you as you think about your action plan?

_____

_____

_____

_____

_____

- How will using a MAP help you make progress towards your desired outcome?

_____

_____

_____

_____

- What is motivating you to achieve this goal?

_____

_____

_____

_____

_____

_____

- How does this goal align with your vision for yourself, your family, and your community?

_____

_____

_____

_____

_____

_____

- How does the MAP align with your values and core strengths?

_____

_____

_____

_____

_____

_____

_____

- What are you doing today to ensure that you are growing where you are planted?

_____

_____

_____

_____

_____

_____

At this point in our journey, whether you realize it, you've already accomplished a great deal. You've learned about your values and strengths, and you've used those insights to develop a MAP. You've begun to PLANT your future.

GRATITUDE *Moment*

Celebrate your hard work with a gratitude moment. We will use gratitude moments to celebrate our accomplishments. List a few things that demonstrate and express gratitude to you at this point.

_____

_____

_____

_____

_____

_____

_____

_____

_____

_____

_____

_____

NAVIGATE OBSTACLES

...A time to get, and a time to lose; a time to keep and a time to cast away...

Ecclesiastes 3:6 (NKJV)

We've been focusing on planning and preparing to plant a bountiful life. Unfortunately, creating a garden doesn't just involve planting and harvesting. We have to nurture and navigate towards the harvest. Cultivating a garden consists of tending to it every month of the year and preventing problems from impacting or slowing the plant's growth. I've learned that nurturing and cultivating a garden requires navigating the obstacles that can undermine or destroy my harvest. During the winter months of snow, ice, and blustering wind, a thick layer of mulch protects your plant's roots, allowing them to rejuvenate in the spring. To ensure a reliable harvest, I have to weed, mulch, and control pests, bugs, and diseases. It's a process that requires considerable attention.

Similar to a garden needing constant attention, so do your goals and dreams. This section will explore the PLANT process by focusing on navigating obstacles that may prevent us from nurturing ourselves. The PLANT process helps you plan, leverage resources, take action, and navigate obstacles to transform plans and goals into a more vibrant life.

As military spouses, we are continually facing challenges and unexpected situations that cause delays, setbacks, and detours to our plans. The constant cycle of new orders, the demands of TDYs, caring for ill, injured, and wounded friends and family members make plans for immediate and future goals complex and challenging. Working on longer-term goals like academic goals is challenging when unforeseen and foreseen circumstances occur.

Nevertheless, I want to encourage you to plant your goals and dreams . Put a seed in the ground and start nurturing your future. Honestly, I never would've earned my advanced degrees, launched my consultancy, established a philanthropic foundation, or created a back-yard retreat for my family if I waited for suitable situations and circumstances.

A wintery hazy, misty fog had settled across Germany, and in my mind. The Spouses Club asked me to facilitate an action board work-shop for several deployed spouses and their teenage daughters on post. It was February, so I decided to weave the theme of love into the workshop. Over the next few days, as I outlined the approach I wanted to take during the work-shop, I kept returning to 1 Corinthians 13.

I always felt this scripture was telling us how we should love someone else, our spouse, our children, our brothers, and sisters. But, day after day of sitting in front of the fireplace, looking at my snow-covered garden bench, I realized this scripture is also telling us how to love and nurture ourselves. Like I nurture my garden seedlings, I can nurture myself and bloom into the women of my dreams. While journaling, I began to explore how I could nurture myself and navigate the circumstances, obstacles, and setbacks of my life to achieve my goals. These five elements can be applied to nurture ourselves and navigate towards our goals.

- Make Room to Grow

- Manage the Weeds

- Build Support Networks

- Persist

- Adapt and Overcome

Make Room to Grow

If you're like me, your life is busy, and your schedule is probably frequently double-booked. Some days, it probably seems like every minute of the day is scheduled or devoted to some task or scheduled commitment. I think we often confuse a busy life with a full life. As I was rushing along the pathway, arms full of grocery bags, I noticed that the hydrangeas I planted along the path, next to the hostas were not thriving like ones I planted in the backyard. I was frustrated; I planted them at the same time. I was tending to them at the same time in the same way. Looking more closely, I saw that the chrysanthemums I also planted along the walkway were crowding the hydrangeas. Then, I thought, "You have to make room---a space for the hydrangeas to grow." I needed to reorder things so the hydrangeas could grow and expand—thrive and flourish. It was an "ah-ha" moment not about gardening but my personal and professional priorities too. I needed to reorder the plants in that section, so my most important priority, lovely pink hydrangeas along my front walkway, could establish themselves and grow.

Similarly, I began to understand, for example, that if my business was going to grow, I was going to have to devote more time to focus on developing my business network or growing my social media presence and submitting contract proposals. If I want to lose weight, I have to make time for exercise and meal planning. Pruning competing priorities is often easier said than done. It takes honesty and discipline to look at our choices and actions objectively and begin to make room for our most important goals to grow and materialize. Once our dreams start to form and grow, they will expand and fill the spaces we provide.

Manage the Weeds

Anyone who gardens knows that weeds are insidious and invasive. Weeds spread fast, and they can choke out your flowers. I've also learned that weeds are often more resilient than my plants. If you don't remove the weeds' roots, they tend to come back time and time again. Weeds reduce crop yield and quality. I've also noticed that weeds spring up during the rainy season, when conditions prevent us from regularly and proactively tending our garden. Simply, weeds must be removed.

Our military lifestyles' transient nature creates an environment for fast, often superficial friendships, based on the common need for support networks, stability, and a sense of community. Let's face it, none of us are resilient enough to manage deployments, frequent TDYs, and PCS transitions while raising our families and pursuing careers without support and friendships. We are indeed in this together at this point. But we have to develop relationships that nurture us, not undermine our growth and development.

You will recall that in the Action stage of the PLANT process, we consider the resources, challenges, and obstacles we may encounter as we achieve your goals. These obstacles have to be navigated, and in some cases, eradicated so we can achieve our goals and harvest our future desires.

Weeds often remind me of "'Friendemies." You know, who friendemies are, these are the folks in your life who show up as friends, but show out as enemies. They are not supporting or encouraging and nurturing you or the plans you have for yourself. If you don't remove them, they can choke off your ideas and success. Sometimes, often during the process of moving towards the plans you've laid out for yourself, you will have to weed out some behaviors and relationships that no longer align with current plans. Remember, sometimes, people enter your life for a particular season. Once that season passes, the relationship may need to end as well.

Sometimes, we plant the wrong seeds in our life. Occasionally, we want to be healthy, but we end up eating sugary desserts. Sometimes, we want to write a book, but we waste time watching television, surfing the internet, and texting with our friends. We also have to make sure that we plant seeds to get the results and outcomes we want. When we don't produce a harvest, we need to adjust by pruning and assessing our environment and actions again.

Frequently check to see how and what things are growing in your environment. If you do not see the growth you expected or anticipated, pull out and remove the weeds or anything else that threatens or undermines your harvest and growth opportunities.

Build a Support Network

I make frequent trips to my neighborhood nursery, and I visit my neighbors' gardens for advice. My tomatoes and cucumbers were an untamed rotting mess until my neighbor showed me how to build support beams.

I would love to tell you that my company became successful because I worked hard, produced engaging communications campaigns, and beat my competition with my business acumen and natural talent. It didn't happen that way, not at all. My business grew because a network supported me. While I spend countless hours refining business proposals, most of my clients find me based on word of mouth referrals from other clients.

My husband, my mother, and sorority sisters encouraged me to start my business. I worked with a leadership coach to hone my interpersonal communication skills. As I described in the previous chapter, relying on the Small Business Administration's business development resources and the Syracuse University V-WISE program, I learned the essentials and mechanics of business development and operations. I hired a financial planner who helped me use my savings for business capital. My former employer became my first client, and she referred me to several other national nonprofits.

Similarly, throughout my career, the companies that I had worked with invited me to submit joint project proposals and contract bids, giving me immediate access to annual contracts, relationships, and opportunities. It honestly took a village of support to launch and sustain my consultancy. I still collaborate with many of the same business partners and clients.

I've needed advice and counsel along the way to becoming an entrepreneur. I needed support, encouragement, guidance, and even some accountability along the way. I needed experts, friends, coaches, and mentors to launch and sustain my business.

It's trendy now for everyone to talk about having a "squad." Whether you build a squad or network, be sure to surround yourself with people who are also pursuing similar goals and plans. Pursue and maintain relationships that create a network of friendships, support, and resources to support you throughout your initiatives and life circumstances. Seek out people who will nurture you and help you navigate obstacles and challenges and those who will help celebrate and support your success.

Some of the plants in my garden can stand on their own. Others, like large tomatoes, need support beams to flourish. When you are planting seeds, the time to build support beams is when the garden bed is small. Frankly, if I didn't use support beams for my business, I don't think my business venture would have survived and thrived during our first two years of operations. My company expanded quickly, and I was able to take advantage of additional opportunities because I had a network of support and resources. My support beams helped me weather storms and made many challenging tasks more manageable.

An essential caveat to building a network is to diligently select and include people in your network who can provide honest, authentic, frank, and constructive feedback, especially in areas when you may need to improve or change unproductive behaviors. Include people in your network who can engage in honest regular conversations with you. These individuals help with accountability and often help break down the silent suffering we may be experiencing. Build these relationships based on trust and mutually shared objectives. Surround yourself with individuals who are pursuing or who have pursued similar goals. My women's entrepreneur and professional author groups often provide this kind of feedback and support for me.

Persist

I fell down a steep hill while I was trimming tree branches in our backyard. I landed on the walkway so hard that a few days later, a knot grew on my head, and my arms and shoulders were black and blue. I had no desire to garden after that fall. My bruises, including my bruised feelings, lasted for several weeks. I needed to cut those tree branches back so I could create a sunny spot to grow some herbs and vegetables in the garden. I began to miss the physical challenges of working in the garden. I realized that I could come back from a setback. I decided to think about how I could prevent myself from falling down the hill next time. I need sun in the garden, so I would have to be persistent. I had to climb back up the hill and cut down those tree branches. My setback became an opportunity to make improvements and persist using another approach. Soon enough, I found myself carefully climbing back up the hill once again.

Persistence simply means that we find a way to continue the course of action whenever we experience obstacles, challenges or setbacks. I had to be persistent over four years to complete my doctoral studies. I worked full-time and went to school full-time to complete my required coursework and dissertation. When I had exhausted my savings to pay my tuition, I took on more and more student loan debt, never stopping to think about the payments I would have to begin six months after my hooding ceremony. It required persistence to earn my degree because I moved twice during the process. A member of my dissertation committee decided to retire, and I had to adjust the timeline to defend my dissertation. The only way to achieve your goal is to be persistent. Let me keep it real. As a military spouse who wants to achieve goals, you must be persistent as you endure TDYs, deployments, military moves, and encounter stereotypes about military spouses, and the military community.

I know the gravity of saying goodbye to a loved one for a deployment. I know the challenges and sheer persistence it takes to reintegrate post-deployment. It is exhausting, and it can be overwhelming. But what we can control and influence is how we respond, react and perceive these situations and circumstances. Keep your thoughts focused on taking action. Success seldom comes easily or without some form of persistence. Allowing your goal to motivate and drive you is one reason the PLANT process begins with devoting time and effort to determining your values, vision, and goals. Persistence is required to keep going when you experience setbacks or obstacles. Use your goals and vision to motivate you. Make your action plan a focal point in your life and devote energy and time toward reaching it.

Achieving our goals requires that we continuously persist, learn new skills, welcome change, and continually look for ways to incorporate new things into our lives. Opening up to new experiences and perspectives allowed me to embrace our PCS to Germany in ways that enhanced my life through travel, cultural exchange, and exploration.

We've all been knocked down and fallen. We've all experienced disappointments and setbacks. But what matters is not the fall or the unrealized expectation. When we persist and navigate the obstacles, we are less likely to die on the vine, get stuck or give up on our efforts and plans. Once we plant a goal or action plan, we have to persist navigate obstacles to ensure we arrive at our destination.

Adapt and Overcome

I purchased some chrysanthemum flowers for the garden. I was rushing when I got home, once again loaded down with packages, and I casually left them near the spiral stairwell leading from the garage to the garden. A week later, I found them, wilting, dried out, and nearly dead. Undeterred, I pruned them, and I planted them, believing that they would bloom once again later in the fall. I was confident they would adapt and overcome my neglect.

Remember, earlier in the book, when I wrote that my cancer diagnosis caused me to fear that I would never have children. Well, shortly after our wedding, we did indeed get pregnant. I began a silent conversation with my son. I would talk to him while driving to work, in the shower, and while I prepared his nursery. In response, he spoke to me too, kicking and rolling around in my womb and causing me to reject every ounce of food that I tried to consume. The first time he kicked, we were sitting in the chapel at Tuskegee University, and the Golden Voices Choir began singing. Soon enough, my mother and mother-in-law started knitting sweaters and sending books. Nightly, my husband read, "If You Give A Mouse a Cookie" and "Oh The Places You Will Go" to my growing belly. We would spend hours sitting on the couch, watching in awe as my stomach rolled as our son, Joshua David tossed and turned.

Like all parents, we began to make plans. We started a college fund so Joshua David could attend Tuskegee University, as his father had. One evening my husband came home with a baseball glove. My mother and sister began knitting blankets and sweaters. One night, as I climbed into bed in my ninth month of pregnancy, I felt a violent flurry of kicks, and then I felt nothing. After a sleepless night, I called my doctor and requested an appointment. An ultrasound in the doctor's office, and repeated in the emergency room, did not detect a heartbeat. He was gone.

We had relocated to a new duty station, so we didn't have any family or friends in the immediate area. My mother drove 10 hours and arrived just as my induced labor was beginning. Reaching forward, I released and delivered my stillborn child in a silent birthing room with my husband, my mother, my doctor and two nurses at my side. Until then, I didn't know that grace and sorrow could inhabit the same moment. With tears, I willed my doctor to do something, do anything to make him cry. Slowly, he shook his head, saying no and then, he silently cried with me.

My husband's Commander and squadron members came—all of them. The Chaplain came. These men who had seen combat and stood on the fight line, held me and cried with me throughout the night. Sharing my pain with them made my son, who never took a breath on this earth real and alive. In the middle of the night, my mother-in-law and Joshua's intended Godfather drove from St Louis.

The next morning, I told my mom and husband that I couldn't return home to an empty nursery. I kept asking them where I was going to go when I left the hospital. The nursery, like my empty womb, held the lost hopes and dreams for my son. I was afraid of that empty nursery. I remember our First Sergeant asking me if they could donate everything to some mothers-to-be on base. He said others had a need, and anything we gave would be helpful to an enlisted family. I thought yes, God please, yes, that this something good we can do, help someone. Help. Make it go away. Quickly. I left the hospital with a few wisps of my son's hair and his footprint. The Air Force was shipping his body home for his memorial service. I didn't open the door to my son's empty nursery.

My spiral began after the memorial service. My mourning was deep. I couldn't sleep at night, so I started wandering the neighborhood and shopping at the 24-hour Walmart in the middle of the night. I didn't return to work. The silence was consuming me. After he was gone, no one wanted to talk about him. I needed to talk about him and to him. In my journal, I tried to resume my conversations with my son. I felt that God was silent, too. I spiraled further down. I wasn't taking care of myself, and I thought that I had developed pneumonia. I went to urgent care and ended up being admitted into the hospital. Eventually, a cardiologist came into my room, sat on the bed, and held my hands in his hands. Looking in my eyes, he said, "Eugenia, you either have postpartum cardiomyopathy (heart failure induced by pregnancy), or you have broken heart syndrome. Both can kill you". He continued, "Your heart is functioning at 10% capacity, you are actively dying. I need you to try to work with me for 48 hours...you will live or die in the next 48 hours". I remember thinking he had the gentlest eyes I had ever seen.

Then I thought, "Well damn." "Isn't it enough, when will it be enough. I gave my son how much more do I have to give? How much farther can I fall? How in the hell did I end up here? Me?". I was confused. I was frightened. I needed to make a choice, as my doctor said. To survive my son's death, I was going to have to adapt and overcome.

Later in the evening, the Chaplain and our First Sergeant came to see me again. They gave me a handwritten note from the young Airman who had received the furniture and clothes from Joshua's nursery. She wrote about how having those things had eased her burden and had brought her family joy. Out of my life's greatest sorrow, someone had been able to experience joy. For a moment, I saw this situation through her perspective; I decided to adopt her view that my circumstances eased her burden.

I needed my son's life, not to be marked by tragedy, sorrow, and death. I needed his life to make a difference. Sitting in that dingy hospital room hooked up to all those machines, depressed, broken, and near death, I cried out and asked God to help me make my son's life matter. I can't remember whose idea it was, but we decided to honor Joshua David by creating a memorial scholarship foundation, The Joshua David Gardner Memorial Scholarship Endowment. The Endowment, established in June 2006, provides scholarships to students pursuing undergraduate degrees at historically black colleges and universities. We've provided scholarships for over 30 students. Our fundraising efforts have been so successful that we were able to establish a second memorial scholarship fund at Tuskegee University.

My cardiologist says that we will never know if it was postpartum cardiomyopathy or broken heart syndrome. I continued to talk to the Chaplain over the next few months. Eventually, I returned to work. To my husband's great relief, I stopped wandering around Walmart at night. I write letters to my son when I need to. My Air Force children call me on Mother's Day to make things easier.

My longing for Joshua is present every day. I'm able to endure this harrowing situation because I shifted my perspective from what was missing and adapted to what I could gain and accomplish through Joshua's Foundation. Our scholarship recipients perform well academically, and they have become entrepreneurs, veterinarians, architects, teachers, and doctors. Once I defined my goal and understood its importance to me, I could redirect and adapt my attention and focus on achieving the goal rather than focus on my challenging situation.

We are always going to experience challenges and unexpected circumstances and consequences while working to achieve our goals and plans. The PLANT process helps us navigate obstacles and unforeseen events, by making room for growth, creating networks of support, being persistent, and adapting to and overcoming situations and circumstances.

I want to encourage you to identify two or three reliable coaches, mentors, or professional contacts that can assist and support you. Implement a plan of action to add some support beams to your network. Write the names of two or three people who can help you navigate obstacles and challenges or lend their expertise to your network.

Building a Network

Person Name & Email	How Can This Person Provide Support to Me

How will I Engage or Connect with this Person	This Person will be a Mentor, Coach, or Professional Contact

"But Moses' hands became heavy; so they took a stone and put it under him, and he sat on it. And Aaron and Hur supported his hands, one on one side, and the other on the other side; and his hands were steady until the going down of the sun."

Exodus 17:12 (NKJV)

- What does the scripture mean to you?

_____

_____

_____

_____

_____

_____

_____

_____

- What do you need to weed out of your life, so you can grow and progress to your goals?

_____

_____

_____

_____

_____

_____

- If you've encountered obstacles and challenges, what can you do to get yourself back on track?

_____

_____

_____

_____

_____

_____

- How are you being persistent in pursuing your goals, regardless of unforeseen situations and circumstances?

_____

_____

_____

_____

_____

_____

- How would love and joy and success bloom in your life if you were patient and kind with yourself?

_____

_____

_____

_____

_____

_____

GRATITUDE *Moment*

How have you made progress towards your goals recently?

_____

_____

_____

_____

_____

_____

Make a list of 5 things you are grateful for in your life?

_____

_____

_____

_____

_____

_____

_____

TRANSFORMATION

And sow fields and plant vineyards, That they may yield a fruitful harvest.
Psalm 107:37 (NKJV)

So far, we've used the PLANT process to prepare for our future by understanding our values and core strengths. We've leveraged our values and strengths to access resources and relationships, and we've developed MAPs to guide us toward our goals. We learned to navigate obstacles we invariably will encounter as we pursue our goals and action plans. In this section, we discuss the final step in the PLANT process, where we harvest and experience transformation and transition. Transformation and transition means that we are beginning to reap a harvest and experience the bounty of planting and working with our MAP. Harvest time, the time of gathering in the crops, is my favorite time in the garden.

Harvest season signifies the end of a process that sees gardeners cultivate and tend to their crops, spanning from the initial sowing of the seeds through to the moment the resulting bounty is ready to be gathered. My house is filled with the scents of flowers and fresh herbs and tomato sauce simmering during harvest season. It's a glorious time at our home. Harvest time is when gardeners will know for sure if their growing season has been a success.

Transitioning to a fuller life experience is a process, not a final destination. Like seasonal changes, it's a constant cycle. The PLANT process helps us engage and maneuver through these cyclical changes, moving us towards our desired goals and outcomes. Let's explore some behaviors that can help us lead more transformational lives.

Of course, there are many avenues to transformation, but I've noticed these five reoccurring caveats throughout my experiences:

5 Core Components to Transformation:
- Be open to unexpected and unplanned possibilities and opportunities

- Engage in life-long learning

- Break from the pack

- Believe impossible is possible

- Share your wisdom and encourage others

Be open to unexpected and unplanned possibilities and opportunities.

In gardening, you plant a particular seed to get the crop you want. Of course, it is much more complicated to see the evidence of a harvest in our lives. We live in disruptive times. If you are a military spouse, when you said, "I do," you unknowingly commit to accepting unexpected and unplanned possibilities and opportunities. It doesn't change your heart's love, but it does mean you have already begun the journey to a life of transitions and transformation. Everyone experiences life as a dynamic, chaotic flow. Yet, at any moment, some seemingly random encounter can link our network of experiences to produce an outcome we could never have planned or expected. Unexpected and unanticipated opportunities are still blessings.

My husband and I live in a community in Northern Virginia, where there are several wooded areas with walking paths. Usually, I deviate from the well-worn path marks others have taken. I prefer to take the unexpected, less worn path. While the journey is sometimes uncertain and the way may be rugged, I find the trail often leads to unexpected and beautiful places or things, and I have the rock and shell collections to prove this throughout our home. Sometimes, the final destination is less important than the journey itself. Sure, sometimes I get lost, but eventually I find my way back to the car again, with a bit more confidence and self-assurance. All of my wandering in Germany, Colorado, Alabama, and Virginia have taught me to enjoy life's journeys. Our many PCS drives across the country have allowed me to visit just about every state in the continental United States. Along the way, I've been able to watch the sunrise and set and cast a purple glow over Pikes Peak. I survived hurricanes and tornadoes, and I've worked with three U.S. Presidents and some of our nation's most decorated war heroes, including Medal of Honor Recipients and Tuskegee Airmen. None of these experiences or our twists and turns were part of my action plan, but each experience enriched my life in unexpected ways. While we are working on our goals, we must avail ourselves of unexpected opportunities resulting from life's twists and turns. Sometimes, the harvest and the joy are found in the journeys, not in achieving the goal.

Consider taking a job outside of your professional track or an assignment to a rural location; an unexpected opportunity can offer unforeseen opportunities, if you are open to receiving them. Initially, I pursued my doctoral degree because I wanted to be a university professor. I received an unexpected opportunity to apply for a public affairs position that would allow me to leverage my political, communications, and nonprofit experience. My willingness to explore this unforeseen opportunity cast me towards a fulfilling and rewarding public affairs career. My desire to pivot into consulting allowed me to evolve into my public affairs career. I believe publishing this book will open unexpected and unforeseen professional and personal opportunities. Being open to unexpected and unplanned possibilities and opportunities can result in transformative experiences.

Engage in life-long learning

The joy of learning lies in the process, not the result. When you commit and engage in lifelong learning, you remain curious, open, and continuously grow.[20]

When I find myself in the middle of a personal firefight, I have trained myself to stop and consider that I should be learning about myself or my behavior in that particular situation. For example, from my many health crises, I've learned the importance of rebalancing my work-life priorities to maintain my physical, spiritual and emotional wellness. Professionally, after every campaign or project, my teammates and I prepare after-action reports that include detailed analyses and constructive criticisms of our performance approaches and outcomes,

---

[20] *Canfield, J. (2005). The Success Principles: How to Get from Where You Are to Where You Want to Be. Jack Canfield with Janet Switzer. Element Books.*

creating a continuous cycle of growth and learning for the entire team and our business partners. We use this information to develop innovations, methods, and opportunities. We create a cycle of growth and transformation for our business practices and ourselves.

Most of us have goals and interests outside of formal schooling. Life-long learning requires embracing opportunities to learn. Cultivate a growth mindset and view challenges as opportunities for growth. Life-long learning can involve developing new skills, self-taught study, or learning a new sport or activity, learning to use a new technology, or acquiring new knowledge.

Reflect on what you're passionate about and what you envision for your future. Technology has made life-long learning more accessible and affordable. Identify blogs, podcasts, virtual seminars, and workshops dedicated to subjects, projects and hobbies, or even museums and community workshops. Watch lectures on YouTube, join an industry group, travel, and try new things. Keep a "to-learn" list and put into practice what you learn.

Life-long learning helps us achieve personal fulfillment and satisfaction. Life-long learning and exploring new things improves our quality of life and sense of self-worth because we are paying attention to the ideas and goals that inspire us.

Break from the pack

Sometimes I get crazy ideas. Creating a garden plot on top of the garage in Germany probably fits in that category. Encouraging my sorority sisters to plan a multicultural Get Out the Vote Festival in the middle of a global pandemic and civil unrest probably fits in that category. Sometimes, people cannot see my vision or understand what I'm trying to accomplish. Like me, my goals and aspirations are unique. Not everyone will share or understand your plans, goals, and aspirations. That's okay. Be prepared to break from the pack and pursue your goals alone.

All of the steps we've previously discussed in the PLANT Process, specifically those that help us understand our values, character strengths, and goals, give us the knowledge and courage to discern and plan to achieve our unique goals. As our support network expands and contracts, and our environment evolves and changes, we can achieve our desired outcomes. Transitioning into your harvest season may require that you go it alone at specific points in time. Being true to your goals will provide an enriching, challenging, and transformative process and experience for yourself. The PLANT process empowers you to initiate your transition and transformation.

Breaking away from the pack may mean:

- Pursuing your goals with a small circle of support and encouragement

- Branching out to create new friendships and relationships

- Choosing unexpected opportunities

- Setting aside role expectations and stereotypes

I was in my early thirties when I enrolled in a doctoral program. On Friday and Saturday nights when my friends were hanging out, I wrote my dissertation in the library at the University of Colorado at Colorado Springs or Colorado College—alone. Knowing my goals and their values enabled me to make choices and set my priorities. Since I was working full-time and attending classes full-time, I had to maximize the time that I could devote to completing my writing and research. Hanging out and being hungover was counterproductive to achieving my goals, so I went to the library—alone. Once I established my routine, I didn't feel left out or isolated. I felt content with my choices and circumstances as I progressed toward my goal.

Breaking from the pack often provides the opportunity for innovation and creativity. Lest we forget, the colonies broke away from England and America emerged. The runner that breaks away from the pack often wins the race. Not only can we break away from people and situations, we can break away from pack ideologies, stereotypes, and mentalities about who and what we are and what we can become and achieve. This is where real transition and transformation can manifest. Military spouses, women of color, and women in general aren't monolithic. So let's break from the pack and be who and what we want to be. When I was a young girl, my father would tell me, "A woman's place is in the world" every day. Let's find our places. Let's manifest and transform into the women we want to be unencumbered by others' stereotypes and expectations. Get comfortable being alone and doing things that are important to you by yourself. Use your MAP to chart the way and stay focused on your unique plan.

One fundamental way all military spouses can break from the pack is by not participating in the "Green code of silence" about the issues of financial insecurity, loneliness, depression, and isolation that are so prevalent in our community. Breaking from the pack involves being courageous enough to talk about the isolation and seeking and building pathways to available resources provided by confidential service providers like Military OneSource and the Military Family Life Counselors. Pursue the support you need to bring a better balance to your life. Suppose you want to achieve different or improved outcomes and circumstances in your life. In that case, you can't continue to do what everyone else is doing; silently suffering is not a solution and will not produce an abundant lifestyle or experiences.

Set aside perceptions and stereotypes about the role of military spouses and follow your own goals and interests. Change your mindset about being the same as everyone else. Do different things, not merely to be noticed, but to be the person that people want to connect to because you make a difference. Breaking from the pack may involve creating more shared childcare opportunities, so you have the time and space to pursue your hobbies and interests. Breaking from the pack may mean that you have to branch out and establish friendships and relationships with non-military spouses, allowing you to expand the possibilities in your life. Breaking from the pack could involve staying in place rather than moving to the new assignment so you can complete your academic degree or professional internship. Breaking away from the pack consists of looking at your unique situation and circumstances and taking actions that support you and your reality.

Believe the Impossible is Possible

Someone I love very dearly has a traumatic brain injury from his time in the service. He has shrapnel in his brain; if it moves at all, he won't survive. To look at and talk with him, you would never know he lives with a time bomb in his head and soul. He's overcome so many situations that the medical professionals said were insurmountable. He carries a photo from when he received his Purple Heart Medal surgeries at Walter Reed Medical Center. He's a bruised, bloody, bandaged mess in the picture. He said he carries the photo to remind himself and the veterans he works with that the impossible is possible.

My other friend was one of a few in his platoon to survive a firefight in Afghanistan. Several of his brothers-in-arms-died. He's fought back severe depression and post-traumatic stress disorder to become a father, entrepreneur, and nationally renowned advocate for all veterans.

My girlfriend's son has multiple personality disorder and schizophrenia. She's facing a dire financial situation as she seeks to secure continued care for her adult son. She called me recently and said that when she talked with her son about their situation, he told her, "to believe the impossible was possible."

Life often presents us with situations and circumstances that you may feel are impossible. As a marketing and communications professional, my teammates and I often find ourselves rewriting scripts, speeches, and storylines. Usually, we reframe the storyline. For example, budget cuts become mission-centric realignments. Workforce layoffs become reallocations of workforce resources. Similarly, we can also reframe our story. Sometimes, we have to flip the script to make the mission possible. Deployments can be an opportunity to develop new friends, gain a sense of autonomy, or acquire new home improvement skills. I know, I'm oversimplifying some of the complex and protracted challenges we face as military spouses. Despite these challenges, we can create a paradigm that provides a more conducive environment for growth and transformation.

No matter what seeds I plant in the garden, I believe they will produce fruits and vegetables. I apply the same beliefs as I PLANT in my life, too. I tell myself my business will grow. I take action to ensure its growth and viability. I believe with practice my proficiency in speaking Spanish will improve, so I can have meaningful conversations when I travel abroad.

Impossible is an opinion, not a fact. They said a man would never walk on the moon. Neil Armstrong did. They said an African American would never be President of the United States. Barack Obama was elected President of the United States, twice. I packed a 5,000 square foot house for a short- notice move in 48 hours, though admittedly, the moonwalk thing was much harder to accomplish. I've survived breast cancer, heart failure, and the stillbirth of my son. My point is that nothing is truly impossible. So, go ahead and dream big and achieve big. Your mission, should you choose to accept it, is possible. Want to transform your life from stress to success or from sorrow to joy? Choose mission possible by seeding a project or an idea that matches your passions, interests, and values. Harness your enthusiasm and believe that with your knowledge, network persistence, everything is possible. Use the PLANT process to make complex and difficult goals more manageable.

Evaluate whether you've prepared for the outcome you are seeking, check to see if you are leveraging your values, core strengths, resources, and relationships to help you achieve your goals. If your MAP has stalled, explore how you can engage your network, mentors, or create new interim goals to correct or re-launch your efforts. Determine what resources you need to leverage to get back on track. Navigate obstacles and setbacks as new learning opportunities, take advantage of the challenge to innovate, grow your network, or establish a new partnership and relationship to address the unexpected situation. Double-check to make sure you are planting the seeds to yield the outcomes you want to achieve. Welcome the impossible as challenges and opportunities to grow and transform your knowledge and yourself. The PLANT process can help you maneuver the impossible towards the possible.

Share your wisdom and encourage others

Each of us has the opportunity within us to create an abundant and full life. Today, we can stop postponing our dreams of earning a degree or turning our hobby into a business. Taking one small step and planting one seed to achieve your desired goal, can inspire others to do the same, allowing you to impact our community and the world.

As you transform into the person you were meant to be and move closer to achieving your goals, others will notice your joy, success, and positivity. Others will be inspired to model your actions and begin to pursue similar goals in their own lives. Be generous with your wisdom, and share your experiences as a way to encourage and nurture transformation in others.[21] For example, I intentionally plan and seek opportunities to speak at conferences, write articles, and conduct workshops because I know sharing my business success and personal challenges will encourage other military spouses and women of color to explore similar opportunities.

My sorority sisters and I decided to celebrate Earth Day by refreshing the landscaping at the USO Warrior Center at the Landstuhl Military Hospital in Kaiserslautern, Germany. We invited the community to join us in creating a community garden. Within a few weeks, we secured enough donations and volunteers to proceed with the Earth Day event. One of the USO volunteers was a master gardener, and she showed all of us, including the wounded warriors staying in the barracks how to prepare and plant the garden beds around the USO center that day. By sharing some of her knowledge, she empowered others to explore their interests and expand their gardening knowledge. We created community through the act

[21] *Canfield, J. (2005).*

of service and sharing. Sharing wisdom opens doors in your life for receiving more -- for yourself, and to share with others.

Sharing your wisdom is one gift everyone can give—freely. You don't have to shop for it, wrap it up, or ship it. Mentoring, sharing your experiences over coffee or on a social media platform are all valid options. Through my business, I frequently offer pro bono workshops or free coaching sessions. These types of activities transform not only my world and sense of contentment, they create a harvest field of support, and they plant engagement, encouragement, and empowerment for others.

We are working for a bountiful harvest. Transformation requires that we are open to unexpected and unplanned possibilities and opportunities, engage in lifelong learning, be prepared to break from the pack, believe the impossible is possible, and share our wisdom and encourage others.

Transformation is the natural evolution of engaging in the PLANT process. Just remember that transformation can be as challenging as it is rewarding. The cyclical nature of the transformation process is supported by continually applying the PLANT process in your life. Consistency is key to creating and maintaining momentum towards your goals and abundance. It's the little things you don't do that stop you from having the life transformation you've always wanted.

The PLANT process empowers and equips you to plant new thoughts, beliefs, opportunities, and actions in your life. Plant something new in your life. Break down planting into these simple ideas: prepare, leverage, take action, nurture, and transform. Using this process, you can plant and sow new opportunities and awareness in your life. Enter the fertile fields of life with seeds, knowledge, commitment, and determination. Once you experience a harvest, continue to PLANT new seeds of opportunity to sustain a cultivated life.

"But Jesus looked at them and said to them, "With men this is impossible, but with God all things are possible."

Matthew 19:26 (NKJV)

Evaluate where you are in the PLANT process using this transformation Model. Use the PLANT worksheets in the Appendix to propel you into continuous growth and transformation.

_____

_____

_____

_____

_____

_____

_____

_____

What impossible goals are you making possible?

Do something or take a risk and try something out of your comfort zone. Rather than avoid something that makes you uncomfortable, embrace it! Write about what you learned in the process and how you felt.

_____

_____

_____

_____

_____

_____

_____

_____

_____

_____

_____

_____

_____

"Stand at the crossroad and look, ask where the good way is, and walk in it, and you will find rest for your souls."

Jeremiah 6:16 (NKJV)

What is this scripture telling you about your current season?

_____

_____

_____

_____

What season are you currently experiencing? Explain why you feel you are in this particular season.

_____

_____

_____

_____

_____

_____

What current opportunities are you facing during this season?

_____

_____

_____

_____

_____

How can you apply the PLANT Process to continue your transformation?

_____

_____

_____

_____

_____

What seeds or plans do you need to put into your next PLANT Process?

_____

_____

_____

_____

_____

GRATITUDE *Moment*

Celebrate your hard work with a gratitude moment. We will use gratitude moments to celebrate our accomplishments. List a few things that demonstrate and express gratitude to you at this point.

_____

_____

_____

_____

_____

_____

_____

_____

_____

_____

EPILOGUE

PLANT: A CULTIVATED LIFE

The doormat on our front porch says, "Home is in the garden." No matter where your military journey takes you, I pray that the PLANT process helps you produce a vibrant garden of joy, love, opportunity, and abundance for your family and yourself. I pray that you grow wherever you are planted.

Thank you for spending time with me planting and cultivating the lovely gardens of our lives. I know you've begun to experience a harvest from applying the PLANT process in your personal and professional life.

As you continue to plant seeds of opportunities, I want to invite you to join our virtual communities on Facebook and LinkedIn, The Garden Spot. The Garden Spot is where we will continue planting and growing, finding the support, advice, and resources to become our best selves. Creating a community is essential to maintaining our momentum toward our goals. The online community allows us to dismantle the isolation and uncertainty by creating a community of spouses that empowers, encourages, and engages with each other. We will share our experiences and celebrate together. You'll get all of the tools and support you need to create a beautiful living garden. I bet we will even swap recipes and share photos of our military families.

At the Garden Spot, you will experience:

- PLANT workshops where you'll receive additional information and support on applying the PLANT process to transform your life

- Direct access to PLANT process resources

- Personal coaching

- Fun and engaging discussions with a global military spouse community

- Early registration access for upcoming special events and speaking engagements

The Garden Spot is for you if you want to continue to plant abundance and opportunities in your life. Join us if you want more joy, purpose, and abundance, and if you want to play an active role in creating a better future, and be a force for good in the community.

Together, we will continue to unleash our capacity to achieve our goals and create beautiful life gardens. Meet me in the garden.

Join me in the garden at

www.eugeniagardner.com

Additional Work Pages

APPENDIX I
PREPARE VALUES
STEPPING STONES WORKSHEETS

Determining Values Stepping Stone Worksheets

Group Your Values (1-5 Groups)				
Values 1	**Values 2**	**Values 3**	**Values 4**	**Values 5**

Values Rank & Importance Matrix			
Rank Top Values	**Why Value is Important to Me**	**How do I Act Upon or Demonstrate this Value**	**How Can I Incorporate My Values in My Life Through My Actions and Decisions**

Character Strengths Summary			
Character Strength	**Summary Meaning**	**How can I use this Strength**	

Action Board Areas of Focus

       Personal

       Social

       Spiritual

       Physical

       Profession

Action Board Digging Deeper Reflections

- What common themes do you see on your action board?

_____

_____

_____

_____

_____

_____

_____

_____

- How do these goals align with your strengths and values?

_____

_____

_____

_____

_____

_____

- What surprises you about your action board?

_____

_____

_____

_____

_____

_____

_____

- What do your current actions tell you about your vision for your future?

_____

_____

_____

_____

_____

_____

_____

- What do you have to change to achieve the goals or plans in your action board?

_____

_____

_____

_____

_____

_____

_____

My Action Plan (MAP) Worksheet

My Values:

_____

_____

_____

_____

_____

_____

My Character Strengths:

_____

_____

_____

_____

_____

_____

_____

My Action Plan		
	Essential Actions	**Milestone & Timelines**
Goal 1		
Goal 2		
	Resources	**Progress**
Goal 1		
Goal 2		

Building a Network

Person Name & Email	How Can This Person Provide Support to Me

How will I Engage or Connect with this Person	This Person will be a Mentor, Coach, or Professional Contact

Plant Transformation Cycle

   Evaluate where you are in the PLANT process using this transformation Model.

Prepare

_____

_____

_____

_____

_____

_____

_____

_____

_____

_____

_____

_____

Leverage

_____

_____

_____

_____

_____

_____

_____

_____

_____

_____

_____

_____

_____

Action

Navigate Ostacles

_____

_____

_____

_____

_____

_____

_____

_____

_____

_____

_____

_____

_____

Transformation

_____

_____

_____

_____

_____

_____

_____

_____

_____

_____

_____

_____

_____

24 CORE STRENGTHS

© Reham Al Taher. 2020 Positive Psychology

THE 24 CHARACTER STRENGTHS
#OtherPeopleMatter

 Appreciation of Beauty & Excellence

 Forgiveness

 Kindness

 Perseverance

 Bravery

 Gratitude

 Leadership

 Prudence

 Connection/ Purpose

 Hope/ Optimism

 Love

 Self-Control

 Creativity

 Humility/ Modesty

 Love of Learning

 Social Intelligence

 Curiosity

 Humor

 Open-Mindedness

 Teamwork/ Citizenship

 Fairness

 Integrity

 Perspective

 Zest/ Enthusiasm

Made in the USA
Columbia, SC
02 September 2021